D1551221

The Wounded Knee Massacre

CORNERSTONES OF FREEDOM™
SECOND SERIES

Elaine Landau

13733

Children's Press®
A Division of Scholastic Inc.
New York • Toronto • London • Auckland • Sydney
Mexico City • New Delhi • Hong Kong
Danbury, Connecticut

Photographs © 2004: Brown Brothers: 3, 5 bottom, 8, 45 center; Corbis
Images: 21 (Bettmann), 30 (Mathew Brady Studio, Medford Historical
Society Collection), 15 (Alexander Gardner/Bettmann), 27 (J.C.H. Grabill),
28 left, 31, 32, 36, 45 left; Denver Public Library, Western History
Collection: 23 (D.F. Barry, B-396), 10 (Northwestern Photographic Co.,
X-31367), 14 (B-705), 20 (F89196); Hulton|Archive/Getty Images: 24, 34,
35; Library of Congress: 9, 44 left; Minnesota Historical Society/George W.
Scott: 26; Nativestock.com/Marilynn "Angel" Wynn: 22, 44 right (Denver
Historical Museum), 39 (Georg Trager/Library of Congress), cover bottom,
cover top, 11, 28 right, 40, 41, 45 right; Nebraska State Historical Society,
Photograph Collections: 18, 33, 37; Nevada Historical Society: 12, 44 center;
North Wind Picture Archives: 4, 6, 13; South Dakota State Historical
Society, State Archives: 38 (Elaine Goodale Eastman Collection), 29;
State Historical Society of North Dakota: 25; Stock Montage, Inc.: 5 top
(Newberry Library), 7, 19; Superstock, Inc.: 16.

Library of Congress Cataloging-in-Publication Data
Landau, Elaine.
  The Wounded Knee Massacre / Elaine Landau.
     p. cm. — (Cornerstones of freedom. Second series)
  Includes bibliographical references and index.
    ISBN 0-516-24244-X
    1. Wounded Knee Massacre, S.D., 1890—Juvenile literature.
2. Dakota Indians—Wars, 1890–1891—Juvenile literature. 3. Wounded
Knee (S.D.)—History—Indian occupation, 1973—Juvenile literature.
[1. Wounded Knee Massacre, S.D., 1890. 2. Dakota Indians—Wars,
1890–1891. 3. Indians of North America—Wars.] I. Title. II. Series.
E83.89.W68 2004
973.8'6—dc22
                                                          2003023889

1 2 3 4 5 6 7 8 9 10 R 13 12 11 10 09 08 07 06 05 04

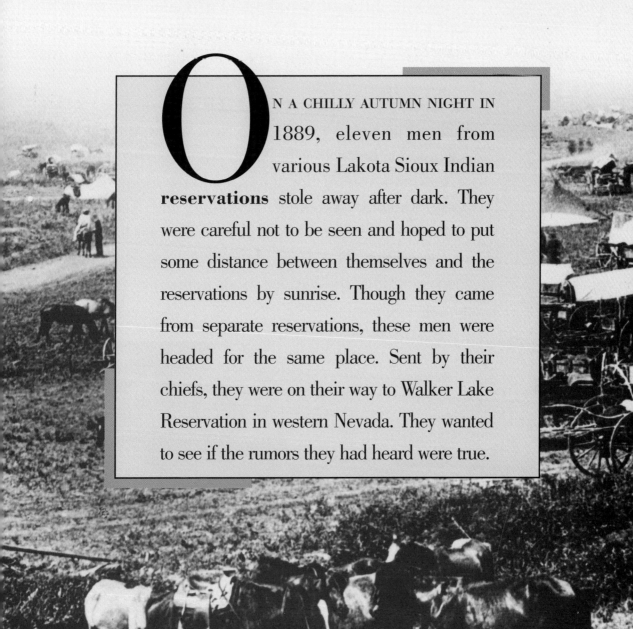

ON A CHILLY AUTUMN NIGHT IN 1889, eleven men from various Lakota Sioux Indian **reservations** stole away after dark. They were careful not to be seen and hoped to put some distance between themselves and the reservations by sunrise. Though they came from separate reservations, these men were headed for the same place. Sent by their chiefs, they were on their way to Walker Lake Reservation in western Nevada. They wanted to see if the rumors they had heard were true.

★ ★ ★ ★

For months, hopeful news had been spreading among the various bands of the Lakota Sioux Indians. It centered on a Paiute **shaman** called Wovoka. Supposedly, during a total **eclipse** of the sun, Wovoka had a vision. The vision promised better times for all Native Americans. At this point in their history, the Lakota could only hope that it was true.

A LOST WAY OF LIFE

Before Europeans came to the New World, the Lakota Sioux occupied a huge area in North America. It included much of the land area of the states we know today as North and South Dakota, Wyoming, Montana, and Nebraska. These Indians were hunters who followed the vast herds of buffalo in the region. The Sioux depended heavily on buffalo for food, clothing, and various other items.

A Sioux village in the mid-1800s

4

This painting by Karl Bodmer shows a herd of bison on the upper Missouri River. Bodmer traveled the American West in 1832–1833 and made detailed paintings of his observations.

THE NORTH AMERICAN BUFFALO

Two hundred years ago, between 40 and 80 million buffalo roamed free in North America. Yet by the late 1880s, these majestic beasts had nearly become extinct. Millions of buffalo were killed by settlers as well as hunters who shot these animals for sport. After 1900, the number of buffalo began to increase, mostly in parks and wildlife sanctuaries where they were protected by law.

This way of life changed in the 1850s and 1860s, when European settlers began to move west in large numbers. The Europeans wanted to settle and farm the land that had always belonged to the Indians. For the most part, the Europeans didn't like or respect the Indians. They thought of them as inferior and they did not honor the Indians' claim to the region.

White settlers killed buffalo for trade and sport. In some cases, the U.S. government encouraged the killings as a way to defeat Native Americans, who depended on the buffalo for food, shelter, and other things.

The U.S. government continually made and broke treaties, or agreements, with the Indians whenever it wanted more of their land. The Indians, in turn, staged attacks to defend what was theirs. They enjoyed a few victories but were unable to make the Europeans leave.

5

U.S. Cavalry soldiers attack a Sioux village.

Actually, the Indians never had a chance. They were fighting against the U.S. Cavalry, a military unit in which the soldiers are on horseback. The U.S. Cavalry was better armed and equipped than the Indian forces. They sought out and killed thousands of Plains Indians. Many of them were women and children who were there when the soldiers attacked Indian camps. Numerous others died from European diseases such as **cholera**, measles, smallpox, and influenza.

The Indians who survived were eventually forced by the U.S. government to live on small, undesirable land areas in North and South Dakota. These areas were known as reservations. In many cases, the Indians were told to farm land on which nothing would grow. No longer

* * * *

able to hunt buffalo, the Indians had to depend on the U.S. government for food as well as many other needs. Often, however, the **allotted** food and supplies were of the poorest quality or never arrived at all. The Sioux spent the winter of 1888 freezing and starving. They knew things would not get any better. The eleven Sioux men who left their reservations in the autumn of 1889 were heading to see Wovoka out of desperation.

The men did not return until March 1890. All the while their people patiently waited for them. Eagerly seeking a new source of strength, these Lakota Sioux hoped that the

Native Americans wait in line to get their share of food and other supplies from U.S. government officials.

men would bring back a plan to set their lives on a better course. They were not disappointed. For many, the answer came in the form of a new religious **movement** that the Europeans referred to as the Ghost Dance.

A NEW RELIGIOUS MOVEMENT

Upon returning, the men told of their glorious days with Wovoka. They said that Wovoka had seen the future in his vision. He promised that one day, the Whites (Europeans) would disappear and all the Indians who had been killed by Whites would return to life. There would again be open spaces, green grass, and plentiful buffalo herds. As in the past, the Indians would be able to practice their religion and customs. They would no longer be pushed onto reservations and would be free to live as their people always had.

Many Native Americans dreamed of a new life, away from the poverty and hopelessness of the reservations.

* * * *

This illustration by Frederic Remington shows men and women performing the Ghost Dance.

The Indians had to take some steps for the vision to come true. They had to stop fighting among themselves and act like a truly united people. That meant finding a peaceful way to settle the conflicts that sometimes arose among the different groups. They also had to do a dance the Europeans called the Ghost Dance and sing special chants and songs described as Ghost Songs. Kicking Bear, representing the Miniconjou from the Cheyenne River Reservation, was among those who had gone to hear Wovoka. When he returned he spoke to his people. "My brothers, I bring you the promise of a day in which there will be no White man to lay his hand on the bridle of the Indian's horse . . ." He went on to tell them what Wovoka said God had told him:

GHOST DANCE SONG

This Ghost Dance song describes what the Indians' world would be like according to Wovoka's vision:

> The whole world is coming,
>
> A nation is coming, a nation is coming,
>
> The Eagle has brought the message to the tribe.
>
> The father says so, the father says so,
>
> Over the whole world they are coming.
>
> The buffalo are coming, the buffalo are coming,
>
> The Crow has brought the message to the tribe,
>
> The father says so, the father says so.

9

★ ★ ★ ★

Chief Kicking Bear (left) is shown here with two other Sioux chiefs, Young Man Afraid of His Horses (center) and Standing Bear (right).

The Earth is getting old and I will make it new for my chosen people, the Indians, who are to inhabit it, and among them will be all of their ancestors who have died ... I will cover the Earth with new soil to a depth of five times the height of a man, and under this new soil will be buried the Whites ... The new lands will be covered with sweet-grass and running water and trees, and herds of buffalo and ponies will stray over it, that my red children may eat and drink, hunt and rejoice.

Wovoka's Ghost Dance vision soon turned into a new religious movement. Native Americans throughout the

* * * *

Great Plains and northern Rocky Mountains felt that the Ghost Dance was their last hope. Anxious to regain their freedom and independence, they started following Wovoka's teachings. They performed the Ghost Dance ceremony in their own languages. Often they added elements of their own group's culture and traditions.

During these ceremonies, the Ghost Dancers wore special garments. The men wore white cotton or buckskin shirts that were brightly painted at the neck and waist. The shirts also had feathers on the sleeves and symbols painted on them. These symbols represented things the wearers had seen in their visions. The women wore white cotton robelike dresses with long sleeves. Like the shirts, the dresses also had symbols and feathers on them.

The Lakota Sioux believed that the Ghost Dance costumes kept them safe. Wovoka had told them that the White soldiers' bullets would bounce off these garments. They could not be killed while wearing them. Though the clothing was supposed to protect them, the Ghost Dance was not a war dance. At no time did Wovoka tell his followers to arm themselves or prepare for battle. The Ghost Dance movement was one of hope rather than of bullets and arrows.

Ghost Dancers believed that special shirts like this one would protect them from harm.

WOVOKA

Wovoka did not always live among Indians. After his father died when he was fourteen, he lived with a White family and took the name Jack Wilson. During that time, he became familiar with Christian teachings. The Ghost Dance reflects various elements in Wovoka's background, including Christianity. Some have compared the rebirth of the Indian people to the rebirth of Christ.

Wovoka told his followers to do no harm to anyone and that they would be rewarded with freedom.

UNFOUNDED FEARS

Unfortunately, many Whites did not understand this new religious movement. They felt certain that the Indians were preparing to attack. White settlers living near reservations where the Ghost Dance was performed claimed to be terrified. They told officials that they might have to flee from their homes if action to suppress the Indians wasn't taken soon.

In some cases, these settlers signed a **petition** asking the United States government for help. They wanted troops of U.S. soldiers sent in to control the Indians and put an end to the Ghost Dance. Thirteen White families from South Dakota signed the following petition:

We the undersigned settlers of eastern Mead County, South Dakota, and the United States of America, do hereby ask in humble prayer for military protection during the trouble . . . [with] the Sioux Indians . . . residing in the villages along the Cheyenne River, from the forks down to Cherry Creek. We ask in most humble prayer, and further demand that we have protection of our lives and our children's and our homes and our property.

White settlers who lived near the reservations wanted the U.S. government to take action against the Indians.

In 1888, President Grover Cleveland created the Second Sioux Commission to break up the Dakota Nation. Pictured below from left to right are Major James McLaughlin, the Standing Rock Reservation Indian agent, and commission members Reverend William J. Cleveland, Judge John V. Wright, and Captain Richard Henry Pratt.

For the most part, the government agents managing the Indian reservations felt the same way. In their eyes, the Ghost Dance ceremonies were a dangerous outlet for the Native Americans' despair. The agents wanted it stopped, and some felt that the Cavalry would have to be brought in to do it. Daniel F. Royer, the agent at the Pine Ridge Reservation, described the situation in a telegram to government officials in Washington, D.C.:

Indians are dancing in the snow and are wild and crazy. I have fully informed you that the employees and the government property at this agency have no protection and are at the mercy of the Ghost Dancers . . . We need protection and we need it now . . . nothing [less than] 1,000 troops will stop this dancing.

Royer was not always worthy of trust, however. In fact, officials in Washington, D.C., often didn't take his claims seriously. Nevertheless, newspaper reporters from around the country soon flocked to

People throughout the country believed what they read in the newspapers, often resulting in an unrealistic fear of Indians.

the area to see what the excitement was about. They quickly picked up on the fears expressed by settlers who believed that the Ghost Dance had put them in danger. Some were more interested in writing an exciting story that would sell lots of newspapers than in reporting the true facts. Often the articles were extremely **racist**, and reflected the newspaper's own **prejudice**. Indians were frequently described as ruthless, bloodthirsty savages rather than as a people whose survival was threatened.

It was reported that settlers in North Dakota were abandoning their ranches out of fear of Native American attacks.

Unfortunately, many of these stories added to the settlers' fear of an Indian uprising. Before long, the press helped bring an already tense situation to a boil. For example, on November 16, 1890, the *Chicago Tribune* published the following article:

> *Settlers on the farms and ranches south of Mandan are fleeing their homes, believing that an Indian uprising is at hand. They urgently demand protection and many a farmhouse in*

16

North Dakota will soon be deserted unless the settlers receive some assurance that they will not be left to the mercy of the murderous redskins, who are now whetting their knives in anticipation of the moment when they begin their bloody work. The Indians are trading their horses and all other property for guns and ammunition . . .

A similar story appeared in the *Omaha Bee* on November 27, 1890. It read:

The chances for blood and trouble generally are as good today as they were a week ago . . . I, for one, of the correspondents here, propose to continue to warn the public that there is still grave danger from many thousands of the Indians at Pine Ridge Agency . . . Will we ever get out of this with our hair? Or, will we get out of it at all?

Although some voices tried to stop the growing panic, no one seemed to pay much attention. Among these was *The Chadron Advocate*, a newspaper in Nebraska that wrote:

It is hard, after visiting the Pine Ridge Agency, to write with patience of the liars, big and little, who have filled the

TROUBLESOME HEADLINES

Newspaper headlines served to heighten tensions between the Whites and Native American Ghost Dance believers.

These are just a few examples:

From the *Chicago Daily Tribune*:

"In A State of Terror"

"Indians Dancing With Guns"

"Fighting Expected at Any Moment"

From the *Omaha Bee*:

"With Rifle on Back"

"The Redskins are Dancing the Dreaded Ghost Dance"

Some reporters visited the reservations to uncover the truth. They found scenic hillsides filled with teepees (right) and orderly Indian schools (opposite page).

continent with scare headlines and inflammatory reports in the past two weeks . . . We left the Pine Ridge Agency Wednesday afternoon. It is a peaceful, orderly, well-behaved place . . . Indian babies and children filled the streets. Soldiers were washing their garments and hanging them out to dry. The smoke of a thousand teepees rose in the still, hazy air: twice a thousand ponies

* * * *

*grazed on the sunny hillsides. There was peace
at Pine Ridge, whatever might be at the homes
of the frightened settlers and in the great newspaper offices.*

Nevertheless, feeling the pressure of a possible Indian uprising, the U.S. War Department reacted. In November 1890, the department began sending troops to occupy reservations where the Ghost Dance appeared to have taken hold. By early December, about one third of the U.S. Army

had been assigned to this task. The public expected them to do what the reservation agents and the local police could not do. They were coming to stop the Ghost Dance.

THE GHOST DANCE TOOK HOLD

By the summer of 1890, the Ghost Dance movement had spread throughout the Sioux reservations. Kicking Bear's people eagerly welcomed him back to the reservation after he'd seen Wovoka. The Miniconjou Sioux became firm believers in the Ghost Dance ceremonies. Most of the Native Americans there were women whose husbands,

The U.S. government sent soldiers to the reservations in an effort to stop the Ghost Dance.

Kicking Bear visited the Standing Rock Reservation, shown here, to spread the message of the Ghost Dance.

fathers, brothers, uncles, and sons had been killed by White soldiers. The idea of having their loved ones come back to life was especially appealing to them.

Kicking Bear and others helped spread the Ghost Dance to still more Sioux reservations. Wanting to bring it to the Standing Rock Reservation, Kicking Bear spoke to Sitting Bull, who was chief there. Sitting Bull did not believe that all the Indians who had been killed by the Whites would be coming back to life. But his people felt differently. Many Indians at Standing Rock had heard of the Ghost Dance and wanted to be part of it. While they respected Sitting Bull's wisdom, they didn't want to be left out if Wovoka's vision proved to be true.

21

SITTING BULL

Sitting Bull (right) was a famous Hunkpapa Lakota Sioux leader known for his bravery. He fought against the U.S. Cavalry in a number of battles. When he was no longer able to hold out against the Whites, he was forced to live at Standing Rock Reservation in what we know today as South Dakota.

* * * *

Sitting Bull was in a difficult position. He did not want to disappoint his followers. However, he knew that the Whites were determined to wipe out this growing Native American religious movement. Sitting Bull feared that some of his people might be hurt or even killed if they became Ghost Dancers. Kicking Bear assured him that everyone would be safe. He explained that even if the soldiers tried to stop a Ghost Dance ceremony, the Ghost Dance costumes would protect the Indians from the Cavalry's bullets.

Sitting Bull decided not to cut off his people from the Ghost Dance movement. He invited Kicking Bear to stay at Standing Rock Reservation for a while. During his stay he was to teach Sitting Bull's followers about the Ghost Dance.

Unfortunately, Kicking Bear's presence at Standing Rock did not go unnoticed by the government agent in charge. James McLaughlin was the agent at the Standing Rock Reservation. He was extremely suspicious of both Kicking Bear and the Ghost Dance. To make matters worse, McLaughlin and Sitting Bull had disliked each other for years. Fearful of the problems Kicking Bear might cause at Standing Rock, McLaughlin sent a group of Indian reservation police to remove him.

Agent James McLaughlin (center) kept a close eye on Sitting Bull. He later reported that Sitting Bull had "behaved very badly" since 1889.

Representatives of the
Department of Indian Affairs
meet with Sioux leaders.

Although the reservation police worked for the Whites,
they were still Native Americans. This made it hard for
them to remove Kicking Bear. When he spoke about the
Ghost Dance, Kicking Bear seemed almost holy to them.
They did not want to take him by force. Instead, the
reservation police asked Sitting Bull to tell him to go.
Sitting Bull refused to help them, and the police left
empty-handed.

Agent McLaughlin was not ready to give up. On Octo-
ber 16, 1890, he sent in a larger force of police to escort
Kicking Bear off the reservation. They succeeded, but
McLaughlin and the government in Washington, D.C.,

were determined to do even more to wipe out the Ghost Dance at Standing Rock.

To do this, the government tried to separate the Ghost Dance movement's leaders from its followers. Sitting Bull was not a Ghost Dance leader, but he was a well-known and highly respected Sioux chief. That may be why he was mistakenly thought to be of importance in this new religious movement. In any case, his name was added to a list of troublemakers put together by the Indian Bureau in Washington, D.C.

Agent McLaughlin had wanted to get rid of Sitting Bull for years, and he saw this as an opportunity to do so. On December 15, 1890, a police force was sent to arrest Sitting Bull. Arriving before dawn, they broke into his small cabin and insisted that he come with them. A group of his followers tried to stop the police from taking Sitting Bull, and a fight broke

A reenactment of Sitting Bull's arrest was staged for this photograph.

★ ★ ★ ★

out. Within seconds, rifles were fired and bullets began to fly in all directions. Sitting Bull was shot in the head and died immediately. By the time it was over, eight Ghost Dancers and six reservation police lay dead on the ground as well.

ON THE RUN

Sitting Bull's death caused a great deal of **anguish** among the Sioux. They had lost a much loved and respected leader. Also, Chief Big Foot of the Miniconjou Sioux at the Cheyenne River Reservation feared that U.S. soldiers might take even harsher actions. The Ghost Dance was extremely popular at his reservation, and he thought the soldiers might strike there next.

This photograph shows the burial of the reservation police who were killed during Sitting Bull's attempted arrest. Sitting Bull was buried in nearby Fort Yates.

The Ghost Dance was popular among the Miniconjou Sioux, shown here on August 9, 1890.

He was right. On December 17, just two days after the incident at Standing Rock Reservation, Big Foot's name was placed on the Indian Bureau's list. The order went out for his arrest.

Anxious about their future survival, Big Foot and his followers fled to the Pine Ridge Reservation. Red Cloud, one of the last great Sioux leaders, had invited Big Foot and his

In an effort to save himself and his people, Chief Big Foot (left) traveled to Pine Ridge Reservation, where Red Cloud (right) was waiting. Red Cloud had not spoken out in favor of the Ghost Dance movement because he did not want to attract the attention of the U.S. Army.

followers to come to Pine Ridge. Red Cloud knew that Big Foot had been able to bargain with the Whites in the past. Red Cloud hoped that Big Foot might once again use these skills to save himself and his followers after they arrived at Pine Ridge.

On the way there, Big Foot's band met about one hundred Indians who had run away from the Standing Rock Reservation. After the shootout in which Sitting Bull was killed, these Ghost Dancers were afraid that the soldiers would come to **massacre** them. Big Foot agreed to let them go with him to Pine Ridge.

Continuing the journey was extremely difficult for the Miniconjou chief. Big Foot had become ill with **pneumonia**. He was no longer able to walk, or even ride, his horse. He had to try to reach the Pine Ridge Reservation riding in the back of a wagon.

Even that was not possible. On the morning of December 28, the Indians spotted the Cavalry in the distance. There was no time to get away. They would have to face the soldiers. Big Foot ordered that a white flag of surrender be put up in front of his wagon.

By mid-afternoon, Big Foot was face to face with Major Samuel Whitside of the Seventh U.S. Cavalry. The soldiers had stopped the Indians at Porcupine Butte. At that point, they were only 30 miles (48 kilometers) from Pine Ridge and possible safety. Meanwhile, Big Foot's health had taken a turn for the worse. He sat up as well as he could in his wagon and addressed Major Whitside.

The Seventh U.S. Cavalry, shown here, forced Big Foot and his group to go to the army camp at Wounded Knee instead of the Pine Ridge Reservation.

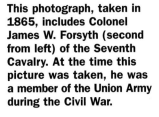

Big Foot explained that he was taking his people to the Pine Ridge Reservation. Major Whitside informed the Sioux chief that he would have to change his plans. Whitside told Big Foot that he had been ordered to escort him and his followers to the army camp 5 miles (8 km) west at Wounded Knee Creek. The Indians had no choice but to go with the soldiers.

THE CAMP AT WOUNDED KNEE

Tensions were high once the Indians arrived at the army camp at Wounded Knee. No one knows exactly how many people were there, but it is estimated that there were almost 500 Cavalrymen and 350 Indians at the site. About 230 of the Indians are believed to have been women and children.

That night, Colonel James W. Forsyth of the Seventh Cavalry arrived at the camp. He made it impossible for the

This photograph, taken in 1865, includes Colonel James W. Forsyth (second from left) of the Seventh Cavalry. At the time this picture was taken, he was a member of the Union Army during the Civil War.

At the hands of the U.S. Army, Hotchkiss Mountain cannons were used to kill large numbers of American Indians throughout the 1800s.

POWERFUL WEAPONS

Rapid-fire Hotchkiss Mountain cannons were powerful weapons. They fired explosive shells weighing more than 2 pounds (.91 kilograms). Those shells could strike a target within a range of 4,200 yards (3,841 meters), or the length of forty-two football fields. If four such cannons were fired at once, about fifty shells per minute would be released.

Indians to escape by completely surrounding them with soldiers. Four rapid-fire Hotchkiss Mountain cannons had also been positioned on a hill that looked down on the camp. The Indians believed that they could be killed at any moment. The Indians' fears were heightened as they watched still more men from the Seventh Cavalry ride into the camp that night. One of the Indians there would later describe the setting in this way:

> . . . I did not sleep that night—did not lie down till morning—was afraid—could not rest or be quiet or easy. There was a great uneasiness among the Indians all night; they were up most of the night—were fearful that they were to be killed . . .

The soldiers were far more relaxed. They were pleased that they had finally captured Chief Big Foot and his Ghost Dance followers. That night they patted each other on the back and

In their tent at Wounded Knee, U.S. soldiers thought that the Ghost Dance problem was about to come to an end.

drank their fill of whiskey. The Indians did not know it, but Colonel Forsyth had orders to take them to the railroad in the morning. From there they would be brought to their new home: an Omaha military prison. The soldiers figured that the Ghost Dance problem was about to be solved.

First, Forsyth needed to get through the night without any trouble. To keep things calm, aid had been given to Chief Big Foot. His health had severely declined. Major Whitside had a small stove placed in the chief's tent and asked the Cavalry doctor to look in on him.

Any kindness shown to the Indians was over by morning. That was when Colonel Forsyth announced that the Indians had to give up their guns and any other weapons they'd brought along. The Indians felt uncomfortable with this demand. It left them with no way to defend themselves if the soldiers turned on them. Some placed their rifles in a pile as instructed by the Colonel, but others held back.

To be sure that the Indians were not hiding weapons in their clothing, Forsyth insisted on having them personally searched. The Indians had to open their blankets and be inspected as if they were common criminals. During this process a shaman suddenly began to do the Ghost Dance. He was trying to remind the other Indians that if the soldiers shot them while they were still wearing their Ghost Dance shirts, the bullets could not harm them.

This proved not to be a wise move. The soldiers didn't understand the words to the Ghost Dance song. They didn't see the song as a form of prayer but rather as a possible call to attack. While they took no immediate action, they remained ready to strike on a moment's notice.

The Indians hesitated to give up their weapons, in case the soldiers turned on them.

At the first sound of gunfire, fighting broke out on both sides.

TROUBLE STARTS

Tensions reached the boiling point when soldiers tried to take a rifle away from a deaf Indian named Black Coyote. Black Coyote had only recently bought the gun and didn't see why he had to give it up. The other Indians felt that Black Coyote could have been talked into giving up his gun. However, the impatient soldiers were not about to

wait. Instead they tried to seize the weapon. There was a struggle, and the gun went off. The sound caused a panic, and fighting immediately broke out between the soldiers and their Indian **captives**.

At the sound of gunfire, the soldiers posted at the cannons on the hill started shooting as well. Some of the Indians tried to grab guns from the pile of weapons they surrendered, but they didn't have enough time. Realizing that they didn't stand a chance, many Indians tried to flee from the camp. Yet they could not outrun the Hotchkiss Mountain cannons. One Indian who escaped told what it was like:

. . . The women as they were fleeing with their babies were killed together, shot right through, and the women who were very heavy with child were also killed. All the Indians fled in these three directions, and after most all of them had been killed a cry was made that all those who were not killed [or] wounded should come forth and they would be safe.

★ ★ ★ ★

Little boys who were not wounded came out of their places of refuge, and as soon as they came in sight a number of soldiers surrounded them and butchered them.

A number of witnesses to the shooting at Wounded Knee were neither Indians nor soldiers. They were newspaper reporters who had come to cover Big Foot's peaceful surrender for their readers. They had never expected to see a battle or, in this case, a massacre. Now they watched in horror as the soldiers fired on the unarmed men, women, and children trying to run from the camp. Thomas H. Tibbles with the *Omaha World Herald* wrote:

Though the active attack lasted perhaps twenty minutes, the firing continued for an hour or two, whenever a soldier saw a sign of life. Indian women and children fled into the ravine to the south . . . but the soldiers followed them and shot them down mercilessly.

Big Foot was one of the first to be killed in the massacre. His body lay frozen on the snow-covered battlefield.

A group of men collected dead bodies from a nearby ravine, where many Indians had sought shelter.

In the end, hundreds of Indians were dead. Twenty-five soldiers died as well. The soldiers put the wounded Indians into wagons and took them to Pine Ridge. But there were no available beds for them there as all the extra space had already been taken up by the Cavalry.

Even though a blizzard was coming, the wounded Indians were left outside in the wagons in the freezing cold for hours. Finally the Episcopal Church was opened to provide some shelter for them. Hay was sprinkled on the floor, and the Indians were set down on it. Tibbles described what it was like in the church:

> *Nothing I have seen in my whole . . . life ever*
> *affected or depressed or haunted me like the scenes*

★ ★ ★ ★

At least thirty-six wounded Indians were treated at the Episcopal Church.

I saw that night in that church . . . Heartsick, I went to . . . find the surgeon . . . For a moment he stood there near the door, looking over the mass of suffering and dying women and children . . . The silence they kept was so complete that it was oppressive . . . Then to my amazement I saw that the surgeon, who I knew had served in the Civil War, attending the wounded . . . began to grow pale . . . 'This is the first time I've seen a lot of women and children shot to pieces,' he said. 'I can't stand it.'

Due to the blizzard, the bodies of those who had been killed at Wounded Knee were left out in the snow for five days. Finally, on January 3, 1891, the 146 frozen bodies were dumped into a mass grave dug at the site. Chief Big

Foot was among these. Black Elk, who lived at Pine Ridge, rode out to the massacre site after hearing the gunfire. He would say of the incident years later:

> *I did not know then how much was ended. When I look back now from this high hill of my old age, I can still see the butchered women and children lying heaped and scattered along the crooked gulch as plain as when I saw them with eyes still young. And I can see that something else died there in the bloody mud, and was buried in the blizzard. A people's dream died there. It was a beautiful dream . . .*

The bodies of 146 men, women, and children were buried in a pit that was dug on a nearby hill.

Today, people still visit the Wounded Knee Memorial in Pine Ridge, South Dakota, to honor those who died in the massacre.

As it turned out, the incident at Wounded Knee was the final military conflict between the U.S. government and the Indians. It marked the end of years of armed Indian resistance. Many of the soldiers at Wounded Knee were given

medals for their role in what the U.S. government called a battle. The Indians, on the other hand, described the incident as a massacre. Today the memory of what happened at Wounded Knee lives on as a shameful page in our nation's past.

Glossary

allotted—given out in portions

anguish—extreme distress or pain

captives—prisoners

cholera—an infectious disease causing serious intestinal disorders

eclipse—the cutting off of light from one celestial body by another, such as when the moon travels between the Sun and Earth

massacre—the brutal murder of a large group of individuals

movement—an organized effort to achieve a goal

petition—a letter signed by many people asking those in power for a specific action

pneumonia—a serious disease affecting the lungs

prejudice—an unfavorable opinion or feeling about someone or something that is not based on facts

racist—having a belief that a particular race or religion is superior

reservations—areas of land set aside for Native Americans by the United States government

shaman—a Native American healer and spiritual leader

Timeline: The Wounded

Eleven Sioux men from different reservations go to Nevada to learn about the Ghost Dance.

MARCH
The men return from Nevada and help spread the Ghost Dance among their people.

NOVEMBER
The War Department sends troops to Sioux reservations to wipe out the Ghost Dance.

DECEMBER 15
Sitting Bull is killed in the fight that breaks out when reservation police try to arrest him.

44

Knee Massacre

DECEMBER 17
Chief Big Foot is added to the Indian Bureau's list of troublemakers.

JANUARY 3
The corpses left at Wounded Knee are buried in a mass grave.

DECEMBER 28
Big Foot's band meets up with the Seventh U.S. Cavalry and is escorted to the army camp at Wounded Knee Creek.

DECEMBER 29
The massacre at Wounded Knee takes place in which hundreds of Indians are killed.

To Find Out More

BOOKS

Bial, Raymond. *The Sioux*. Tarrytown, New York: Marshall Cavendish, 1998.

Freedman, Russell. *Buffalo Hunt*. New York: Holiday House, 1988.

McLerran, Alice. *The Ghost Dance*. New York: Clarion, 1995.

Waldman, Neil. *Wounded Knee*. New York: Atheneum, 2001.

ORGANIZATIONS AND ONLINE SITES

Lakhota Sioux Heritage, Culture, and Language Site
http://www.lakhota.com/home.htm
This Web site offers interesting information about Sioux culture, language, and heritage.

New Perspectives on the West—Wounded Knee
http://www.pbs.org/weta/thewest/places/states/dakotas/ dk_wounded.htm
This PBS Web site features maps, photos, and information about the events at Wounded Knee.

Index

Bold numbers indicate illustrations.

About the Author

Award-winning children's book author **Elaine Landau** worked as a newspaper reporter, a children's book editor, and a youth services librarian before becoming a full-time writer. She has written more than two hundred books for young readers. Landau lives in Miami, Florida, with her husband, Norman, and their son, Michael.

13733